MARY SLESSOR

MARY SLESSOR OF CALABAR

Mary Slessor

THE DUNDEE FACTORY GIRL
WHO BECAME
A DEVOTED MISSIONARY

J. J. ELLIS

JOHN RITCHIE LTD
CHRISTIAN PUBLICATIONS

ISBN-13: 978 1 909803 53 4

Copyright © 2013 by John Ritchie Ltd.
40 Beansburn, Kilmarnock, Scotland

www.ritchiechristianmedia.co.uk

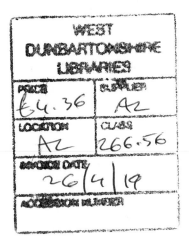
Typeset by John Ritchie Ltd., Kilmarnock
Printed by Bell & Bain Ltd., Glasgow

INDEX.

FOREWORD.

G OD'S grace and Scottish grit make a splendid blend and both account for the character and doings of Mary Slessor. This factory lass, who did so much for Christ, owed all that she was and accomplished to the dour courage inherited from her ancestors, and to the Grace of God that first saved her and then made her dogged to seek to share the blessing she had received. "An achieving life," says an American writer, "is represented as a life in which faith takes commanding place." God's grace gave the gift of faith to Mary Slessor, and faith opened the door of her heart to a long train of heavenly blessings. For every Christian who is humble finds of God that—

He giveth more grace when the burdens grow greater;
He sendeth more strength when the labours increase,
To added affliction He addeth His mercy,
To multiplied trials His multiplied peace.

His love has no limit, His grace has no measure;
His power no boundary known unto men;
For out of His infinite riches in Jesus
He giveth, and giveth, and giveth again.

Perhaps the most satisfactory explanation of her wonderful charm, holiness and power to win souls for Christ, will be that she always stood in God's smile. A phrase explained in the following incident : It is said that many years ago in the city of Chicago a little boy stood in a window through which the sunshine was streaming in such a way that rainbow colours appeared upon his slippers. He was wild with delight, and cried out, "Look Mother, what is this?" She replied, "That is God's smile, and I hope that when you become a man you will always stand in God's smile."

Years slipped past and the boy became a man with a man's duties and love of work. He was industrious, and rapidly acquired great wealth. He built himself a palace-like home, and then set himself to get more money. His mother passed from his sight, and he moved her few possessions to his new abode. He himself opened the trunk in which the special treasures were kept, and saw these slippers upon which the rainbow colours had played. With them was a paper written by her giving an account of the incident. It concluded thus : "I am afraid my William has gotten far away from God's smile. God grant he may return again and stand in the smile of redeeming love in the Sun of Righteousness." The strong man paused in his reading, and after a moment or two of serious thought said to himself. "Yes : far, far—very far from God's smile. But here and now I return and will seek the sunshine of His love until again the rainbow of mercy shows its beauties in my life." He surrendered himself to the claim of God; confessed his sins and forsook them, and laid hold of the promise of mercy given in the Gospel. Having believed and cast Himself upon Christ there came peace into his soul, and at once he began to seek to share the blessing he now received through trusting

Christ. He got rid of his business and employed both wealth and talents to tell to others around what a dear Saviour he had found, and as he did this he came into the splendour of God's smile.

May every one who reads this brief account of a truly Apostolic career resolve not to make a living, but to secure the smile of God and live in the daily consciousness of sins forgiven, and a sure title given to the inheritance of the saints in light.

> The opening heavens above me shine
>   With beams of sacred bliss,
> When Jesus shows His love as mine
>   And whispers I am His.
>
> My soul would leave this heavy clay
>   At that transporting word
> Run up with joy the shining way
>   To greet my glorious Lord.

CHAPTER I.

> 'Tis easier work when we begin
> To serve the Lord betimes,
> But sinners who grow old in sin,
> Are hardened in their crimes.
>
> . . . .
> Who seeks to praise God and to make Him known
> To other hearts must have Him in his own.

"ONE of the deepest instincts of our nature teaches the preciousness of severity," said John Addington Symonds, but it is hard to believe him while the soul stings with injustice, hardship, or pain. Mary Slessor born at Gilcomston by Aberdeen, 2nd December, 1848, was educated under the harshest conditions, but she was kept sweet by the love of God in her frail mother. She had few advantages, and many crushing difficulties, but she shows what can be done by those who have few chances, but who are Christ's, and are willing to be nothing, that He may be glorified. First the lassie was brought out of nature's darkness and at once set to work to carry the light to others, and all her days she went forward carrying the lamp to show everyone the way to happiness and peace.

Her father was a shoemaker, and at times sober, kindly and tender. But he lacked a saving interest in

Christ, and before long became a victim of the drink
sin. Gradually the octopus arms tightened their grip,
and the more they grasped the less the deluded man
desired to be free.

Mary's mother was one of those sweet, frail women
for whom a bad man has a fascination. The
mothering instinct is useful but it can be perverted
as it was in this case, for that husband grew the worse
the more he was loved.

Like all children the little maiden often played at
keeping school But her supposed pupils were all
of the black, for even at that early age the missionary
instinct was strong within her. And no wonder. She
was cradled in love for missions, and longed to take
part in the blessed work of telling others about the
Lord Jesus, the mighty to save, and full of love for
the sad. As with all strong natures, there were spells
of wilfulness that now and then grieved her gentle,
suffering mother. In sheer wilfulness she stayed away
from Sunday School. Irritable, she was greatly dis-
turbed when she was called "Carrots" or "Ginger,"
for the reddish colour of her hair.

Instead of whipping the provoking offender, that
gracious mother would pray for her, and this touched
Mary's tender heart. "Oh, mother, I would far rather
that you whipped me than prayed for me so. It hurts
me so that I have given you such pain," Mary said
when these scenes occurred.

Wistful to the call of the Holy Spirit, deeply in-
terested not only in the well-being of her own Church,
but with a keen desire that the Gospel might win its
way in heathen lands, was that mother in whom Mary

found a refuge and, along with mother-love, the Holy Spirit moulded the girl-heart for purposes as yet—far beyond her ken. Mrs. Slessor belonged to the Presbyterian Church, and taught her daughter to hear the cry from Africa, "Come and help us." The planning of the mission to Calabar excited much interest in the shoemaker's humble dwelling, and was talked about as well as prayed for. Thus Mary early acquired a desire to help although as yet she had nothing to give for she had not obeyed the call of God. In spite of the saintly mother, home life was trying, and at times almost unendurable. With the unreasoning selfishness of the drunkard, Mr. Slessor sold his home and transported his family to Dundee, where in the mills, wife and daughter might work in order to keep him in drunken idleness. The proceeds of the sale of furniture were soon swallowed, and then losing his situation the drink slave became a labourer in one of the mills.

At first they had a little garden before the front door, but her father did his gardening there on Sundays to the grief and shame of his wife and daughter.

Seven children called this unworthy man father, of whom four died young and all were frail. The gentle mother took her children where they could hear the story of redeeming love, sent them to Sunday School, and in order to provide them with food went to the weaving mill. Mary in spite of this haunting terror of a father was wild and full of excited vitality. Her conversion came about in the following way : An aged woman, living near the Slessor family in Dundee, was in the habit of getting the young folk around into her house, and speaking to them of God and eternal things.

She did not mince the truth, but told it out faithfully. One cold night, Mary and some other young girls were in this aged woman's house. "De ye see that fire, lassies?" she said, pointing to the fire on the hearth. "If ye were to put your hand into the lowes, it would be sair. It would burn ye. But if ye dinna turn to God, and believe on the Lord Jesus Christ, you will burn in the bleezes of hell fire for ever." These plain words went like an arrow to Mary's conscience. She could not sleep for thinking of them. And the result was, she came as a guilty, hell-deserving sinner to Christ and was saved. Home she went to her mother, and clinging to her in a fond embrace whispered that she had found a Saviour for herself. "So now I'll try and not vex you by wilfulness. Jesus will make me a good girl and a comfort to you." This new bond was a strength to both, and a source of deep joy. Speaking of her conversion in after years, she used to say, "It was fear of hell fire that drove me into the Kingdom." And there are thousands like her. It was to escape the doom that they knew awaited them that caused them to flee to Christ, and when they reached Him, they learned His love and trusted Him, saying, "Who loved ME and gave Himself for me" (Gal. ii. 20). The Bible of course became her constant companion, and from its pages she gathered stores of wisdom and strength. Instead of questioning she read the Holy Book, and then she found that it changed her heart and altered her outlook and doings. As she fed upon its wonderful words she began to love the Lord Jesus Christ as a Saviour, and also as a constant Companion and Friend. Her path was not strewn with roses. One

year after her tenth birthday when many children have
no other employment than play, she went to the mill.
At first she spent only the morning in the mills, the
afternoon she attended school. But soon she was put
on full time. There, from six in the morning until
six at night she toiled amid the whirl and noise of
machinery, breathing polluted air, but the while con-
scious that she was not alone. This life was exhaustive
enough, but before leaving for the mill and on her
return from it, Mary busied herself with household
duties so as to relieve her mother.

And while the tyranny of love compelled her to do
this Mary's mind opened by the Bible began to crave
for more knowledge and yet more. On her way to the
Mill and back home, and while busy there, she picked
up fragments from books, and what she thus obtained
she digested. One trial left its deep scar upon her
heart to the end of life. Saturday nights were dreadful. The children having been safely secured in bed,
Mary and her mother would sit knitting waiting for
the return of the drunkard.   Unreasonable as are
such brutes the creature would fling into the fire the
supper which others had pinched to provide , and
rave as such fellows do. These two trembling victims,
often turned out into the street, kept their shame a
secret and suffered in silence, fearing lest it should
bring scandal upon the church.

At length the reprobate died without any repentance,
perhaps like many, he had so long neglected the call
of God that he had ceased to hear it.

Mary now became the chief support of the home,
she, her sister, and their mother working at the mill.

Mary eventually took charge of two looms—and they were not unhappy, for theirs was toil sweetened by love. The mother exchanged the noisy mill for a small shop in which Mary assisted.

It has been said that character is best seen in the way leisure hours are employed. Mary found her recreation in mission work. Especially the savage lads who warrened in the alleys were her choice. These by her calm courage and persistent faith she won, because through her lips the Christ who dwelt in her heart spoke to them.

Thus the days went by—hard toil, self-sacrifice and earnest and sustained effort to win the worst for Christ. This is a fine training, for when one can bring Christ to others He becomes doubly real and precious to our own hearts, and is better understood.

One night a band of wild boys pounced upon Mary with threats and wild actions. "What do you come bothering us for? Go to your chapel over the shops, and let us alone to do what we like," they cried.

"I will not give up coming to seek you," replied the trembling girl, praying for courage.

"You must, or we'll punish you."

"You must do what you wish, but I must obey Jesus," was the brave answer.

Then a huge lad took a lump of lead at the end of a cord and swung it nearer and nearer her head. It just grazed her forehead, but she stood quite still. The boy threw away the lead, and he and his gang followed her to school.

A brave act indeed, and only possible because Mary loved the Saviour and fully trusted Him. Then she would visit the homes of these children, not heeding either poverty or sullenness. Her sunny ways and gentle spirit soon made her welcome, and she was pressed to come again.

Thus she continued working at the Mission the while she prepared for the greater task that God had in store for her.

Her mother, while she dearly loved her bright, capable daughter, cheerfully gave her up for work in Calabar, no small sacrifice for one who loved so much. The two daughters who remained in Dundee were earning good money, and Mary promised part of her salary to keep the home fires burning. Her love to the Saviour showed her not only to love and help the heathen, but to care for the dear one dependent upon her love and needing her care.

Events are often the voice of God, and His call soon sounded through Great Britain. First came the emancipation of the slaves in Jamaica, which was marked by an outburst of longing on the part of the liberated to carry the Gospel to Calabar, whence many of them had been shipped. The Rev. J. N. Clarke and Dr. Prince were sent from Jamaica to explore and they sailed to the Gulf of Guinea. After making careful enquiries they proceeded to England. But their vessel was struck by lightning and drifted a helpless wreck across the Atlantic. At Jamaica the arrival of the envoys aroused the keenest interest.

Here it may be as well to notice that the Calabar region is now a part of Nigeria. In size the kingdom of France and Belguim cover the same area, and this region has a population of some seventeen millions.

The ocean washes a swampy mass of mud in which grow trees of a kind. Behind this breeding ground of malaria lies a vast country then inhabited by warlike tribes, slave merchants, who stole, and sold human beings with many and filthy cruelties. The population was degraded as might be expected. They were brutal, ferocious, their lives haunted by dreads, and stained by habits, dear as polluting.

This was the land about which Mrs. Slessor had talked, and her children were fired with her enthusiasm and prayed that Calabar should have the Gospel.

In 1875 Mary with the consent of her mother offered herself to the U.P. Foreign Mission Board as a missionary to Calabar. She was at this time 28 years of age. Accepted at once she was sent for three months special training. Then when appointed her salary of £60 per year was divided, the larger portion being left for the support of her aged mother. Her piety was of the kind that delights in love to parents even when poor and of lowly education.

CHAPTER II.

A Loyal Missionary with Ideas and Visions of Her Own.

Nor to the throne from heaven's pure altar rise
The odours of a sweeter sacrifice,
Then when before the mercy seat they kneel,
And tell Him all they fear, or hope, or feel;
Perils without and enemies within,
Satan, the world, temptation, weakness, sin;
Yet, rest, unshaken in His sure defence,
Invincible through His Omnipotence.

—Montgomery.

We must bring great ideas into life—a pure glowing heart; kindling aspirations; the sense of the Divine presence; the consciousness of our spiritual dignity; the large high hope of glory everlasting—and we shall see deep meanings in things which otherwise seem devoid of meaning, and realise splendid treasure in what threatened only weariness and disappointment.

—W. L. Watkinson.

SO at last Mary Slessor was a missionary. With large hopes and a brave heart she left her dear ones for Calabar. Viewing all things with the eyes of love she could not at first believe that with beautiful trees, a sky so clear and blue, gay birds and luxuriance of loveliness all around, the climate was as deadly as she was told it was. It's true, that thanks to her sturdy Scotch training, she was able to walk abroad without a hat, go barefoot through the tangled undergrowth of the forests, but in time she found that tropical beauty is poisonous to vigour and

17   B

activity. She looked at the surface and in like manner
she judged the natives when she at first made their
acquaintance. For thirty years the Presbyterians had
laboured among them, and while a congregation of
a thousand attended the preaching services, only 174
persons were avowed believers in the Lord Jesus
Christ.

A religion the natives had but it was a terror. For
instance ; in order to satisfy the god of the Shrimps
men and women were bound where they must be
drowned, and this was considered an act of religion.

While on probation one of her duties was to ring
the bell at dawn to call the faithful to prayer. Then
too she would run races with the black children,
and even climb trees in the path in the exuberance
of her spirits. Besides these feats she visited among
the people, comforted them in trouble, remonstrating
with them when they were doing wrong. So passed
her apprenticeship, and then she came home on furlough.   She then requested the Board to give her
another station than Duke Town, for in her the
aggressive instinct was strong. They sent her to Old
Town within reach of her training school. Several
small stations quite accessible were placed under her
control. More than this she was able to reach the
natives behind, that were shut by the Calabar people
from contact with the coast.

With Scotch prudence she considered her finances,
and found that if she were to help her mother and
sister, she could not live as did other missionary ladies.
She would not explain her reason for economy but
decided to live in a native hut, and upon the food that

LADY MISSIONARES CROSSING A RIVER

the blacks eat. Her abode, unlike the English homes in Mary's time, was wattle and mud, covered by a roof made of mats.

No idea of cleanliness or sanitation troubled the dirty blacks; but these always follow a reception of the Lord Jesus Christ as King. She soon became known as, "the Ma who loves babies." One day a man brought her a baby he had picked up in the bush. It was a twin, the survivor of two that had been flung out for the wild beasts. Miss Slessor took the child and called it Jeanie, after her sister. Soon other boys and girls found a home with her, for Mary Slessor knew that the heart of the black is as susceptible to kindness as is that of the white, and equally capable of receiving eternal life through faith in the Saviour.

When years grew upon her Mary's bed was placed in the middle of the room. The children were suspended in limp hammocks. To each hammock a string was attached so that Mary could swing them to sleep while herself in bed.

Of course she opened a school and among the scholars sat one of the chiefs, eager to learn, and willing to repeat the lesson with the children beside him on the bench.

Then she would go out accompanied by two boys, who carried a bell. This would be rung, and then public preaching and worship followed. Something in her attracted attention, and loving the theme, she found that John iii. 16 was as sweet in Africa as in Britain, and as full of saving grace.

One custom she found especially evil and deeply rooted in popular esteem. The birth of twins was regarded as a horror and insult. One of the babies was supposed to be a monster, its father an evil spirit. As it was impossible by inspection to detect which was the monster, both babies had their backs broken, were thrust into a water pot, and flung into the bush to be eaten by ants or wild beasts. The unfortunate mother was treated as an outcast, and abandoned to die. This cruelty she rightly supposed to be the consequence of fear, and rescued infants wherever she could. Moreover, she suggested that the Mission should set apart a lady to take charge of the twins that could be saved, but as the Board dare not incur this additional expense, she herself undertook this difficult task.

Then, pitying the tribes shut out from legitimate trade, she afforded them facilities for getting past their opponents, considering that to do this would help to strangle the slave trade.

One visit she paid to one of these chiefs, and was received with great honour. At night all the chiefs' wives came and sat close to her, and as these were corpulent, and perspired freely, dawn was rather a relief to her.

Trouble broke out, as it always does, where Christ is made much of. The young wife of a chief entered a yard where a boy was asleep, and two other girls were privy to this. At once Mary interfered, and succeeded in reducing the sentence of 100 lashes with a cowhide to ten. Then she nursed the wounded girls, whom she could not prevent being beaten.

Before long some new workers were attracted to the Mission, for a real work of God always wins suitable helpers.

Janie being with her while at home in 1884, Miss Slessor found that her sister needed a warmer climate than East Scotland. At first Mary desired to take her to Africa, but this was not permitted. So she took her mother and sister to Devonshire, and fetched a friend from Dundee to attend to their wants. The only sister who could assist died, so that the expenses of the two invalids must be paid by Mary alone. Her mother, with heroic self-sacrifice, would not hold her back, and to Calabar, with tears in her eyes, and the love of God in her heart, Mary went. The native houses there were a trial to a decent woman; while from December to March, there blew a wind that carried fine dust with it, and this shower of drying dust soon withered up the energies already flabby in the damp heat.

After her return from settling her mother in Devonshire a man came to Miss Slessor, and, pointing to little Janie clinging to her skirts, said, "That's my child; I am her father."

"Oh, you have come to see her. Well, of course you will come now and again to see her."

"Oh no," said the man, "I could not come to see her."

"Well you are foolish! What harm can a wee girlie like she is do you? Come along in."

"No, I'll look at her a long way off for fear she hurts me."

At this Ma lost her patience at the man's hard-hearted folly, and taking firm hold of him she pulled him up to the child.

"Janie," said she, "this is your father. Now give him a good hug."

The touch of the tiny arms softened the man. He fondled his child, and his love, now awakened, he could hardly tear himself away from the girlie whom he had left to die in the bush. After this he came frequently to see the toddler, and brought her many gifts. Truly Satan's rule is one of hard hearts, and natural affection dies out where there is no love for God and desire to please Him.

While Janie was in Glasgow she was put into a bath. The child took the sponge and began to schub the soles of her feet, which weren't so dark as the rest of her body.

"Why Janie, what are you rubbing your feet for?"

"Oh because I think the white places are getting bigger, and if I keep on rubbing and soaping perhaps I'll be white all over some day."

Bye and bye came the tidings that the brave, frail mother had passed away, and six months after the sister also went to be with Jesus. This left Mary Slessor alone, so far as relatives were concerned, and hers was a rich nature full of warm love, which longed to lavish itself upon some one. All this was given to the Africans, and fully they repaid the affection that wrapped them round in its soothing embrace. Day and Sunday Schools of course were held. Old and young crowded together and learned first the alphabet, and then to spell. After school, this slight, bare-headed woman, preached and prayed, keeping always the Saviour and His dying love well to the front. Not many dared to avow themselves Christians, but there were some quiet souls that silently drank in the news of God's love and became secret disciples. Judge them not, for they were ruled by ignorant cruelty. The sister of the chief, a great friend of Mary, but a heathen, showed dents on her arm like vaccination marks, and said they were caused by her husband's teeth!

Good was being done, but this restless little woman could not be content while the mass of heathen within reach were still living in filth, brutality and degrading sin.

She longed to carry the Gospel to these savages, realising the risk she ran, but fearing no danger if only the news of God's love could be told to these dusky children of Adam.

Twelve years of quiet service she had spent in Calabar, but she believed in aggression, and had visions of these multitudes in filth, wretchedness and ignorance of Christ and His blessed Gospel becoming obedient to the commands of Christ. This was no dream, for she had received a keen sense of the value of the Lord Jesus Christ, and, living in close fellowship with Him, had come to understand somewhat of His vast purpose and longed to give Him the desire of His heart, and bring these wanderers into His fold.

And should not larger visions of the possibilities of our Lord and His work dawn upon us? Your Sunday School class, family and circle of acquaintance should receive the first and best of your efforts, but take larger views. Jesus is worthy to receive all homage, and the earth He watered with His tears and blood is, after all, but a little gift. Do not rest satisfied with small successes, but press on to greater. Every capture should be an incentive to win some one else for

the Lord Jesus Christ.   During a battle an excited
officer dashed up to Sir Colin Campbell, exclaiming,
"We have captured a standard!"   "Then go and capture another," was the quick and wise reply.   Our
daily breathing should be—

> O that the world would taste and see
>   The riches of His grace,
> The arms of love that circle me
>   Would all mankind embrace.

CHAPTER III.

Still from God's creating hand
New witnesses for Truth shall stand,
New instruments to sound abroad
The Gospel of a risen Lord.

—Whittier.

In thee let love with duty join,
And strength unite with love,
The eagle's pinions folding round
The warm heart of a dove.

—Stanford.

Ever since the perfect man walked the earth, every man of sympathies has been a man of sorrows.

—Stanford.

MARY SLESSOR had with her own consent been appointed to the vast region back of Calabar known as Okoyong. Here she met with a fierce race who had thrust themselves south, and had all the characteristics of conquerors. Physically and intellectually they were much superior to the race they had pushed back, but then they were worse. Intellectualism unless sanctified simply gives greater proficiency in evil. Every thought and purpose should be brought into captivity to the Lord Jesus, or it becomes a centre of putrefaction.

25

These men traded in guns and chains of slaves, and their pursuits degraded them. The importation of rum too had accelerated the corruption evident in all their habits. Rum was the money of the district and the delight of all. Even babies were fed with it; from the cradle upwards it was the solace and ruin of all. Weapons were always at hand and freely were they used at the least provocation.

It was with some dismay that her friends heard of Mary's bold venture.

The King of Creek town, Eyo, had a canoe twenty feet long, and upon the stern he had erected a screen of palm leaves to keep off the sun's rays. She stopped for tea on the way and found that the cup had been left behind.

"Never mind, I'll cut open a tin of stewed steak and the tin will do as a cup," said Ma.

Alas! the boy while washing out the tin dropped it into the river, and she saw it no more.

"Never mind," said Ma, "I've got the saucer left, and that must do."

The King's vessel carried her to the post of danger, and there she found that God had before prepared for her coming. The chief, Edem, gave her a warm welcome, his sister, Ma Eme, became her fast friend. Permission to build was at once granted, and also it was allowed that the right of refuge should be accorded to all mission stations.

Two sites within easy reach of each other were selected and prepared, and the foundations of two churches were made ready.

After a flying visit to the coast Miss Slessor re-

A TYPICAL TRANS-ZAMBESI AFRICAN LADY

turned to Ekenge, her new station, accompanied by Mr. Bishop, a printer. Night had fallen when they landed, and then the party had a four mile tramp through the dense forest. The missionary had a bundle on one arm, a baby boy astride her shoulders and pulled herself along through the dripping tangle of thick undergrowth. At length they reached their destination, and then Mary had to march back to the canoe where the crew were asleep. She tumbled them out, and they without demur carried up her goods. Her headquarters were in the women's yard of Edem's abode. The walls were of mud and so too was the floor. The indefatigable lassie put in window frames and stopped the gaps in the structure with moistened clay; to her, personal comfort was subordinate to the master passion that ruled in her soul. She lived to win souls, white or black, to the peace and comfort she found; and laboured by speech and deed to point them to Jesus the mighty to save.

A slave was to be put to death because he was supposed to have used witchcraft. Ma interposed, pleaded and reasoned, but the savages, yelling out their rage, waved their guns and swords close to her. Her soul was at peace, and hence her demeanour was calm. After a while her God-given courage quieted the shouters; they consented to flog the man and load him with chains. This was not what she wished, but it was some small triumph, for which she magnified God.

Soon after she heard of a chief far away who was dying, and had sent messengers to her. Chief Edem warned her not to go, but she went through the forest, the rain pouring down upon her the while. Flinging aside her damp garments, she went on, and, reaching the scene of trouble, found preparations for slaughter were in progress.

By God's blessing she nursed the chief back to life, and once more rescued helpless sufferers from a cruel death. Then came a worse trial. A drunken chief, who was very cruel, came to visit Edem. As they drank the vile poison sent from Europe, the village became the scene of a wild riot. Ma tried to get the visitors away before there was actual combat. But they spied on the path through the forest some withered leaves and plants lying on the earth. At once they shrieked out that there was sorcery, and wanted to go back to the village they had just passed and kill every living soul there.

Ma rushed in front of the savage host, and stopped them in their rush. It was a daring deed, but it succeeded. The drunken savages took another path, and Ma went back weary but thankful. Alas, the next day the chief came back, and after many acts of injustice in the village seized a young man to be put to death. Ma went and pleaded for the man's life, the while Edem got ready to fight for him, for the village was his. After a while the Lord softened the drunkard's heart, and he released the prisoner; once more Ma had succeeded by the power of prayer.

Ah, we don't realise sufficiently the value of prayer, and fear to ask because our language is feeble or hesitant. But prayer is the Christian's "vital breath," and only as he prays can he live as God accounts living.

There was need of her witness, for man without the Gospel is a savage, cruel, and full of evil likings. Here is an instance :—A man bought a young slave and made her his wife. One day this girl went off to one of her master's farms, and sat down in the hut of a slave. She refused to quit, and the man troubled with vague dreads, went off to his work and left her in possession. Alone with her thoughts, and having no comfort such as Christians possess the poor woman walked to the forest and there hanged herself. The slave into whose hut she had strayed was put in chains and sentenced to death. He was charged with bewitching the woman, which accounted for her coming to his hut and then killing herself.

A fierce conflict ensued but in the end Miss Slessor secured the man's release, the first of many victories she achieved over deep rooted custom and hard callous selfishness.

The while she busied herself with these special efforts Mary held school and preaching services. The school was held at night-time, and was followed by a simple service, where she set forth in loving tones the love of God manifested in the sacrifice of Calvary.

Interruptions and special appeals were frequent, and to these she at once responded. Thus she was sent for to visit a sick chief, and against the advice of her friends (who realised her peril), set off immediately in the pouring rain. Shaping her way through the thickets, various articles of clothing were flung off, but still the little woman pressed on. She found the chief ill, and administered the medicine she had brought with her. More was needed and she sent by a trusty messenger for a further supply, and received with it some tea and other cheering gifts. The fever was upon her but she revived and effected the cure by the blessing of God.

Then Edem, the chief, whose guest she was, fell ill with an abscess in the back. At first this was attributed to witchcraft, and the suspicion was a death sentence to many shivering natives. To escape her appeals for these innocent sufferers the chief moved away to some distance. Then the sister of one of the native pastors nursed him, the abscess burst and he came to a sane mind as his body acquired strength.

While grateful to Edem for his hospitality Mary wanted a mission house where she could be quite free to do her varied work. It was a long time before she could induce the people to move, but at length mud huts with additions at right angles were erected. She herself with Scotch acuteness, constructed a fireplace of clay, and of the same red material a dresser and sofa were formed.

Then she built a church at Ifako, a central position, and opened it with the approval of the chiefs, who promised to send thither their slaves for instruction, and pledged themselves that no weapon should be carried into the building.

Then she induced King Eyo to invite the chief of Okoyong to visit him at Creek Town. The interview was a success and the way was opened for trade as well as for the Gospel. Man, unemployed, tempts himself and degenerates rapidly, while labour is health and Christian work brings a blessing to the soul. Do not dream; be up at once and do something for Christ, and the more every day's toils are consecrated to Him the more will the soul grow in His likeness and favour.

Then came Mr. Ovens, a carpenter, to help her and she constructed a Mission House of two stories for health and comfort's sake.

Then came a tragic interruption, one that threatened to completely stop the work.

The eldest son of her powerful chief Edem, contemplating marriage, was felling a tree for house building. The tree slipped, he received a blow and was at once paralysed. For two weeks Mary nursed him and then he died. Popular opinion at once decided that he had died of sorcery, and a number of men and women from a village near were seized, chained up ready to be put to death. The chief, Akpo, and most of his people escaped. Night and day Mr. Ovens and Mary watched, baffling all attempts to administer poison to them, and at length the massacre was averted, but the chief, now baffled of his murderous purpose, attempted to poison himself.

Another triumph was that Miss Slessor was able to secure the return home of the exiled chief, Akpo, and the reinstatement of him in his property.

Soon after this success she was presented with a canoe, and erected a boat house on the beach so that she was prepared for an expedition by the river so as to reach the distant tribes she longed to see Christians. Gentle as she was with the weak and ignorant, Mary could be resolute enough when she thought it necessary. She has been known to thrust stalwart men back from the drink, and when one of them refused to put down his gun she tore it from him,

and then refused to allow him to come near it.
Another brawny black having applied to her for
medical help she took out the castor oil.   The man
acted like bad children and would not unlock his lips.
She gave him a box on the ear, and when he had been
dosed resumed her usual placid demeanour.   Another
time hearing that a boat loaded with weapons of war
was afloat, she insisted upon the surrender of the
hatchets, and so helped to shorten the conflict.

The while, busy in a thousand sordid tasks, she kept
up her reading feeding her mind with good books,
and studying the Bible as the source of all her comfort, wisdom, and strength.   Hence she was much
in prayer, and by it was made brave.   Thus while
traversing the forests where leopards dogged her steps
she took refuge in prayer and so won courage and
deliverance.

No wonder that her force of character, courage,
and that indescribable charm, the kind always possess,
brought chiefs and even whole tribes to her so that she
might settle their difference, and point out to them
the right path.   The while with counsel she told of
God's love; surely some that heard her plead in after
days tasted that love, and found salvation through
Christ's sacrifice.

Once when packing, weak and ill, she heard that a
young man had died from a gunshot wound in the
hand.   This led to preparations for combat.   Taking
two men with lanterns she went to the danger zone,
addressed the men like bad schoolboys, secured peace,
and although she could not prevent their drinking, she
did her best to shorten the debauch.

In 1891 she came to England, accompanied by her Janie, one of her best girls. Then it leaked out that she was engaged to be married. A young teacher of Scottish birth had fallen in love with her, and as she could not leave Okoyong she wished him transferred to that station. The Board, however, did not think it wise to take the young man from Duke Town where he was doing excellent work, and so the love romance faded away, and Mary Slessor went forth alone, save for the Divine Companion, to do the work He gave her to do.

In 1892 she returned to Africa comforted to know that a training Institute was to be established to educate and evangelise the natives, or such of them as were willing to be Christians.

From quiet England and practical Scotland it was a contrast to return to the home of witchcraft and murder. The chief's sister, Ma Eme Ete, acted as her informant. A certain bottle being sent for physic, was a warning that some wickedness was in contemplation. Then at once "Ma" would set out for the post of danger; it being a mystery to the chiefs as to how she divined their purposes. Now and then when there was strife likely to lead to a fight Miss Slessor would make a scrawl upon some paper adorned with dabs of sealing wax and despatch this paper to the wrangling mob, who were puzzled by it.

During the interminable talks which always preceded a conflict Mary would sit and knit. This helped her and assisted her influence.

Now and then when there was a riot she would order the noisy quarrellers out, and they obeyed her as

C

sheep the order of the shepherd's dog.

After a while the British Government, who had hitherto exercised a shadowy authority, took over the district. The Governor appointed vice-consuls for different districts, but none was required at Okoyong, where Mary Slessor kept things quiet.

From this time began her acquaintance with Government officers, and these were as devoted to her as were the black followers. Many of them did not share her faith but they realised her value, listened to her counsels, and it is to be hoped got glimpses of the Saviour she loved so well.

Besides this the Vice-Consul paid her a visit, and induced the chiefs to promise not to kill slaves at a burial, and to give their twin children to Miss Slessor. The latter pledge was not redeemed, and intent upon securing her purpose the determined Scotch lassie induced the Governor to come himself and counsel order and justice.

So with but little success such as figures in reports, Mary Slessor toiled on neither abating effort nor hope. Happily, sure of her Saviour, she told the tale of Redeeming Love with delight, feeling its force and believing in its unfailing efficacy.

After a while she found that the primitive methods of farming in vogue compelled a movement to lands that had not been exhausted. A town had sprung up at Akpap, six miles from the river, and she urged that the Mission should follow the people to their new settlements. The Board established a Mission station beside the river while Mary, herself, fixed up a hut in the new capital.

RESCUING LITTLE CHILDREN IN DARKEST AFRICA.

An epidemic of smallpox soon after swept across the country and gave her more and unpleasant tasks from which she did not shrink. These and other labours exhausted her and compelled a return to Scotland. She was too weak to walk to the ship; her wardrobe was supplied by gifts from British Christians and so with four black lasses she came to Caledonia to recruit. She was impatient to be at her work, saying "If ye dinna send me back I'll swim back. Do ye no' ken that away out there they are dying without Jesus?" Before long she was back in Africa, as before, alone. But she succeeded in civilizing the district of Okoyong, for she brought Christ and His redemption to bear upon the problems of life. Before long she was not only the judge before whom complaints were made, but also the refuge of the desolate, helpless, and the wronged. She gave them wise counsel, and told them all about Jesus, and His name opened hearts and changed them.

Once only at Okoyong was she in real danger, and the consternation it caused showed her popularity. There was a fight and she interposed to obtain peace. A stick struck her, and at once there arose a cry, "Ma is hurt! Ma is hurt!"

The enraged spectators would have killed the man whose stick struck her had she not pleaded for him. Nor was this the only danger that she encountered and survived. Indeed, her life was one long series of miracles, for the Angel of the Lord was with her as her guard.

On one of her journeys up the Cross river in a canoe with some of her children a huge hippopotamus

attacked them. It snapped its jaws, butted against the
frail vessel, the men beating it and thrusting their
paddles down its throat. Ma prayed and gave encour-
agement to the men, and after a while they got away
from their huge assailant.

Then one of her babies married, but the new life
was not a success, and before long she was back with
"Ma." Then the division of Nigeria into two districts,
each under a High Commissioner, led to military oper-
ations, and Miss Slessor was brought back to Creek
Town until peace was secured.

At length, fifteen years after landing at Calabar,
the first celebration of the Lord's Supper was held,
when the black converts, the fruit of her toil, met
together with her to remember the Lord according to
His commandment.

Suffering as she did from the effects of the climate,
and the long series of privations she had endured
Mary Slessor could not quit. She cast her eyes upon
a bend of the Cross river, a place called Enyong Creek.
A place where of old the great slave market was held,
and where the headquarters of murderous witchcraft
were located. About four millions of human beings
were within reach of this beautiful watershed—the
staple trade of the district being slaves and murderous
religion. The Government sent a military expedition
to deal with the slaves and the dealers, and with
their fall the whole system of wholesale murder received a blow. Mary Slessor fixed her camp at Itu,
whence she could strike out to the regions on either
side with effect. First, she saw to it that her station
at Akpap was provided for, and then made her way

through the trees to the Government launch. The officer commanding the troops induced her to go to Arochuku, where she found herself amidst a dense population of 30,000 souls. Here she planted a station, and on her way back to headquarters was stopped to visit a chief who as a boy had learned a little of the Christian faith. These encouragements to advance were duly appreciated, but she first made good her foothold at Itu. So possessed was she with the idea, that as a woman she was the best possible pioneer into danger centres, that she resolved upon spending her holiday exploring the new country. At the time she was weak, because of her hardships and the food that did not nourish, but the generosity of private friends supplied the funds necessary of the exploring expedition. Her salary at the time was less than £2 per week, but she asked no help from the Mission Funds.

Leaving two ladies at Akpap, she conveyed her family to Itu. Here her new abode was finished, the cement on the floors being spread by her own hands. This was done while deputations from far came to her—her influence daily increasing as she moved about the country forming schools, and in one place leaving a lad of twelve who soon had a large number of scholars under his charge.

Then she was relieved of Itu by a doctor being appointed to the charge, and she went to I Koto bong, a town farther east. Not content with this advance, she longed to plant a station still more in advance, but her cautious committee had to curb her activity. The Government official presented her with a bicycle, and this assisted her in journeying along the new Government roads. Checked in pioneering, she set herself to attempt to provide employment for the women. She desired to buy land in the name of her girls, and use it as a training ground for the women who were not married or attached to a ruling family. In due course it was recognised by her Board that Mary Slessor had great abilities as a pioneer and they allowed her to choose her own methods and stations.

CHAPTER IV.

A Good "Ma," who was also a Great Queen.
A Proof that Love always Conquers.

> He was a man among the few,
>   Sincere on virtue's side,
> 'And all his strength from Scripture drew
>   To hourly use applied.
>
> That rule he prized, by that he feared,
>   He hated, prized, and loved;
> Nor ever frowned or sad appeared,
>   But when his heart had roved.
>
> Give every flying moment,
>   Something to keep in store,
> Work for the night is coming,
>   When man works no more.

IN May, 1905, Miss Slessor was appointed by the District Commissioner to act as presiding magistrate at Itu and its surrounding districts. A salary was offered but refused, yet she accepted the post as part of her missionary work. She was not only remarkably proficient in the native language, but it appeared as if she thoroughly understood the native mind. To this remarkable faculty was added that insight, wisdom and influence that comes from Christ

throned in the heart. Her piety was undoubted but
she remained herself, and expressed her experiences
in her own way, and in characteristic phrases and
actions.

Thus at times instead of sending a convicted offender to prison she would smite him upon the head.
And when the chiefs, who sat with her as assessors,
talked she would warn them, and if they continued
to chatter she would rise from her seat and box the
offender's ears.

Later on she trained her girls to hear the complaints
that came to her, and then from them she gathered
sufficient information to enable her to form her
opinion and give her decision. With all her vigour
and capacity to rule she was gentle to weakness and
kind to the suffering. So as the "White Ma" she became well known all over the district, and a true
mother she was to thousands. The mothering instinct
led her to adopt the hated twin children; to nurse them
as she sat on her rocking chair, while others lay about
the floor wrapped in newspapers or sheets of brown
paper. And the attachment of the rescued did not
satisfy her—she longed to mother all the tribe. As
"Ma" she reproved, resisted, and smote them, and this
was borne because her affection was clearly perceived
by those who came under her sway. Her colleagues
while they saw her with amused admiration, were content to be treated as her children; even Government
officials with no great love for missionaries as missionaries, loved her as a mother and were devoted
and willing subjects of her rule.

Grave officials and chance visitors came under her

spell. To her they were just laddies, to be warned, cheered and loved. The Ma in her was always power-ful. Her loss of near relatives, the spiritual apprecia-tion of the value of every human soul, even of the most degraded, drew forth her sympathy, and she loved because she must do so. Here perhaps would be the best place to insert some letters which at once reveal her simple character and genuine piety.

In the *Baptist Times and Freeman* for November 2nd, 1917, Mrs. Charles Brown writes :—

"I heard lately from my husband that a dear friend of his possessed some letters from Mary Slessor which, if I could obtain permission, would doubtless be of interest to those who have read the life of this courageous pioneer missionary. So I made my way to Barnet, and found Miss Grace Kirk willing to trust me with the precious letters awhile, and to permit me to make such selections from them as I might desire. I think they reveal Mary Slessor's great loving heart in a wonderful way. She and Miss Kirk had never seen each other in the flesh, yet a truly spiritual love sprang into being between them, and this grand mis-sionary found time to put very much of herself into these letters.

"The correspondence began thus : A brother of Miss Kirk's a man of noble Christian character, an engineer, who spent many months at a time on the West Coast of Africa, met Miss Slessor at Calabar.

"On one occasion, after a sojourn in England, Mr. Kirk, on his return to Calabar, took with him a letter and a book from his sister Grace to his friend Mary Slessor.

"In return for these, letter No. 1 found its way to
Miss Kirk."

Ikoi-Obon, Calabar,
September 29, 1906.

My DEAR LASSIE,—What a sweet letter, and what
a precious gift you have sent me—truly a cup of cold
water twice over. Surely the Holy Ghost prompted
the choice both of words in your letter and the message of the book. I had not ever seen the compilation
before, but anything of Tersteegen's is very full of
the savour of His name and spirit.

Oh I am glad that Mr. Kirk has a sister who lives
in the secret place of the Most High. There are
Christians and Christians, and God has chosen to take
you into the inner circle where He satisfies the soul,
satiates His people with the fulness of His House. Do
you know one of our superior officers here has a sister
who knows the Lord like that, and she is such a help
to me, and prayer from such must have greater power
for others as for oneself—so I rejoice that Mr. Kirk
is upheld like this, for life here needs special grace.
Christians are few, and are usually content to be as
little distinct from the world as possible, as there are
few restraints, and few privileges and means of grace.
But Christ *can* keep and can make His people always
triumph, and your brother knows the keeping power
and lives it, and is an epistle of Christ known and read
of all men. It is a great strength to me to know that
he and two or three more are on the Lord's side, for
one gets to feel living alone among the heathen, as if
one were fighting a forlorn hope; then one catches
sight of a fellow soldier and remembers that we are

A DAY-SCHOOL IN DARKEST AFRICA.

one of a host, and that the battle is not ours at all, but the Captain's, and that all we have to do is to obey and follow and triumph.

There have been two or three very sympathetic men here of late, each a son of godly parents and they have been most helpful to my work as well as to myself.

But when I got to know your brother first he was the only Christian I could find in Government employ, and I often prayed for him that he might be made a great blessing to his fellow officers, some of whom have Christian parents who travail for their salvation. I wish I could have you here instead of writing to you. I am going about trying to open new stations, so I have not a settled home, but I can't tell you about it just now as I have a Government despatch to write tonight, and my eyes are blinking.

I had a young Scotch lad, a carpenter, here this week for a holiday and doing a little work for me, and he devoured your book. He knows Christ, not after the flesh, but as a constant indwelling power and joy, and he got "a cup of cold water" too, after a rather trying time. My books are all at my old station, so I long sometimes for a reading of something less ephemeral than papers and magazines, even the best of them, and I've read all I can scrape here. Will you accept my warmest thanks for your gift and your very cheering and sisterly letter, and will you pray that I may represent Christ worthily and truly in these new dark places? Also will you pray that my bairns may all be saved entirely for service and be made missionaries in deed and truth. I have some difficult and delicate work in hand. Will you ask God to give

me all tact and grace and wisdom, and so follow up
your kind gifts? Please write again, and accept tender
and warm affection from yours very affectionately,
MARY M. SLESSOR.

The next letter came eighteen months later in reply
to one from Miss Kirk conveying the news of the
death of her dearly loved brother.

Use Iköl Oku,
February 28, 1908.

MY DEAR FRIEND,—How can I ever thank you sufficiently for such a latter? What it must have cost you
to write it! And yet it is good for you to have done
it, for it will make God's goodness all the more real
to you to put it in form thus; it has certainly been a
great satisfaction to me to know that he was surrounded by your loving care, and that God had kept
him in such perfect peace..... If anything had happened to him out here or at sea, your heart's hunger
would have been dreadful, but He gave him to you,
and you to him, so that his troubled brain could find
peace and rest, and your hearts could pour out their
love treasure on him and then put away the weary
body where you can go and visit its resting-place. "I
will sing of the loving kindness of God for ever," will
ever be the uppermost feeling in every Christian heart
under all circumstances and at all times, and you can
sing it now, and your dear one is in the perfect light
and perfect love waiting for you all. Instead of your
waiting for his furlough and feeling the anxieties of
absence in a trying climate, you can look up and know

that he is nearer than ever, and that there will be no more sickness or sorrow for him, only a higher service, and a joyous, unclouded welcome when the home-going is permitted by the Father. Will you give your mother my warmest and tenderest sympathy and love; she has much to thank God for in having given to the world such a son to witness for Him on this coast where witnesses are few, and where those around him needed all the help he gave them by his life and teaching.

The two gentlemen who called here last week, and who are from Christian homes, spoke so beautifully about his life and its help to them all. It would have cheered you to hear it; those who have Christian homes are bound by a wonderfully strong and subtle tie..... I am writing this as a wee note to say "Look up and trust our Father"; you and I have not begun to explore His grace and fullness yet. "Open thy mouth wide and I will fill it." Drink deeply of His love, nestle closely under His shadow; that is the resting-place, and be often with His Word. What a storehouse the Bible is when the Spirit illumines it.—Yours very lovingly,   MARY SLESSOR.

Letter No. 3 contains at the close a touching picture of one of those home-comings when Mary Slessor brought with her one (on other occasions several) of the babies whom she had rescued from a cruel fate.

Use Iköl Oku Via Itu.
November 11, 1908.

DEAR LITTLE SISTER GRACIE,—So you wonder whether you should write to me and if it would add to my burden! You Dear! You did not remember the other side, that it is such a joy to me to hear from one who loves and serves the Master..... And do you think I shall ever forget the brother who lived so consistently for the Lord that all men took knowledge of him that he had been with Jesus? No, dear; Christians are too few and steady men of principle are rare out here, I hope I shall ever cherish his memory as an inspiration and example.

I thank you ever so much for writing to me, and if you do not get an answer believe all the same that I think of you at the throne of grace and that I hold you in my heart in tender remembrance. You speak of added trials to yours faith in the health of your mother. I may say that I enter into your feelings exactly there, for I remember the first time it came home to me that it was not mother thinking for me, but that I should have to be everything to her. I had come off a journey, and had the oldest girl I have as a baby in my arms. I was tired and wearied in heart, and thought I was to just cast my wee black girlie into her arms and tell out my tale and be comforted, as I used to all my life, when my sister put her finger to her lips and said, "Mother is ill and very queer, but I would not tell you for fear you should be alarmed." And then I went in and found her as weak and as unable to understand anything as the sleepy baby I carried. That was a long illness, and I was at home two years with her, so I know how you feel a wee bit; but I also know that both you and your mother are in perfectly safe and tender keeping and that you will not lack any good thing. If I were you

I should not strive any more after attainment. I **was** like that, and I wanted to realise in my own experience all the heights and depths of Christ's love, and to be able to say what eminent saints could say; but later on I found that to be passive in His love, and just drink it in, and rest in it, and lean on it, and pray in it, was far better and tended more to growth in grace and interest in prayer. The more intense the love the more silent and useful it is.

Now, dearie, I am at the end of my strength. I have had a dose of fever that has given me this half-hour's leisure. I have waited to give baby her drink and she has got it, and so I must lie down, for I am so tired, and to-morrow is Court day. But this scrap will tell you that I love you, and think of you and pray for you—I am, yours in true love and tender,

M. SLESSOR.

The following letter was written about a year before her death and before the great war had broken out, of which she lived to see only the first six months :—

At the Government Rest House.
Ikpe,
9th *February*, 1914.

MY DEAR FRIEND,—I am here doing a little gipsy-ing, and I am to be kept on another day evidently, so must try to get a wee bittie written to you. I have just been reading one of the sweet poems you sent me as a New Year's Gift, the text of which is, "She considereth a field and taketh it," and it is so very much to the point of present circumstances and has given such a feeling to my desire and determination

that I must tell you about it. I am between my two
regular stations—there are fifty miles between—and
I use this resting place when I choose, and my determination these last months has been to make an on-
slaught on several towns here where Satan's seat is.
They refuse to accept God's Word, though they would
like the children to learn to read and write. They
fear the displeasure of their gods, and they fear
having to take twins and twin-mothers into their
towns lest they all die. But I have long been claiming
them for my Lord, and I am going to sit there for a
few days at least, and am taking the A.B.C. card, and
shall try to captivate and interest the children and
young people, by teaching them on the road side, and
so work in that they shall find that God's Word means
not death but salvation. Poor souls! Terror-stricken
in the gross darkness of heathenism, and afraid to go
and meet Him who comes to deliver. . . . My dear
lassie! I had a grand triumph for, and through my
Lord last night in the town. They utterly refused
to look at the card, and to repeat the names of the
letters was very expressly refused; but before we
finished the whole crowd was at it, and when I wished
to stop—as they had been out all day on the farm and
the food was not cooked nor the water carried—they
cried "Go on, ma," and we went at it again, and
several of the biggest lads came home with us talking
seriously of things in general till they became quite
communicative, and we are to meet again this evening.

Then this morning the chiefs have all come, and we
have had every obstacle and difficulty cleared out
thoroughly, and I am to come and teach and preach,

and to do as I like with them. Oh! my sister, I am a
grateful and glad woman this morning! and I just
pass it on to you, to tell you to try and help us to win
through, by joining us in prayer that the prey may
be taken from the mighty.

Miss Slessor was keen to mark the signs of secret
or coming blessing; she knew that God was working
on behalf of the work of the Mission. Hence she
rejoiced when there was in Scotland a growing recog-
nition of the value of woman's activities, among the
savage tribes. Her own tact, self-denial, courage and
wisdom in ruling disarmed the hostility of the wicked
to the claim of Christ. Alone amongst those who set
not the least value on human lives, she carried no
weapon, save her tongue, had no lock upon her doors,
yet she ruled brawny warriors and compelled them to
listen to the message that she was never too tired to
utter. She told them that God loves man, and that the
Lord Jesus Christ died to save them, and that trusting
Christ and accepting Him as Saviour brings peace
with God and happiness among men.

Another indication of the Holy Spirit's gracious
activity was the appreciation of the value of artisans
who could handle tools, the while testifying to Christ.
The besotted rum drinker who did not care for the
Book would listen with respect to the man who could
build houses or work in iron. It was thus in the first
days that the Gospel won its way. It stole into fami-
lies because servants talked of it; it came with the
workman, and while he wrought at his craft it softened prejudices and opened ear-gate to the Spirit's call.

One trial was that the blacks had no sense of the

D

value of time. They took but one meal per day, and were willing to spend hours in useless talk, which often boiled up in anger.

She herself knew no cessation to her toils. When busy with some needful task she would hear the cry, "Run, run Ma!" and off she would rush to save the innocent and interfere on behalf of the suffering and weak. To her came slave parents to tell how, denied necessary food, the master had carried away their child threatening to kill it. A long and wearied negotiation followed, but it ended in the child being restored and the parents sent back to work. Her career is remarkable because she took risks that were fatal to others. She had no filter and drank the water of the district without first boiling it; never wearing a hat she went without shoes or stockings along paths where snakes and jiggers abounded.

Her study of the New Testament was one explanation of her methods and safety. A passionate and persistent love for the Lord Jesus Christ mastered her and all she did or bore was for love of Him. She believed that He could take care of her, and He did.

Now and then when she felt the need of Christian comfort she would take her children with her, and sure of a welcome make her home in a Mission House. When the occupant was a bachelor, the wise thing was to let her sleep with her babies on the floor. Eccentric though she was, Mary Slessor was very human, and longed for companionship and the solace of a friend. Choking down the sorrow that surged up she would set herself to stir up all she knew to attempt great things for God, the while busying herself in menial

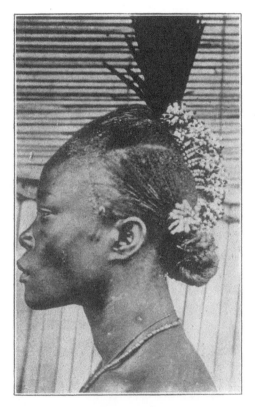

A LUBAN LADY

and exhaustive toils. One incident will show her determination. A band of women were thrust into a yard by valiant warriors who intended to kill them. Miss Slessor stood before these soldiers and through a whole day and night she kept them from killing. When a storm of rain and wind cooled these doughty soldiers, she crept secretly back to her house to find that the stock of condensed milk was exhausted. Her mat roof had been carried off by the storm and neither clothing for the wet girls or milk for the babies could be procured nearer than at Calabar. Carrying a baby soaked as she was, Mary reached Creek Town, slept for one hour, and then returned with changes of clothing and tins of milk. No wonder that dysentry laid hold upon her.

Dr. Laws, the founder of Livingstonia, the Scottish Industrial Mission on Lake Nyassa, came home on furlough in 1891. He prepared a booklet explaining the aims and essentials of the Mission, to whose success he had contributed so nobly. One essential was that the buildings should be erected upon hilly or rising ground with pure water and good timber within easy reach. The second was that while aggressive effort to reach the heathen with the Gospel was essential with them, there should be a training institution to educate native workers to spread and establish the work. The pamphlet was widely read and absorbed by the thoughtful. It suggested that if Livingstonia were such a success would not a similar mission be useful in Calabar, where the need was so acute? Dr. Laws attended the Committee meeting, and it was suggested that he should go to Calabar to investigate and report upon the course to be adopted.

Accompanied by the future Superintendent of the proposed Institution, in July 1892 he went to the West Coast of Africa. Three months were spent in the Calabar district—months of enquiry, prayer, stimulus and healing of both mind and body. During the rush of this work there came a letter from Miss Slessor saying that war was threatened, and that she was laid aside with dysentery. Knowing her spartan fortitude, that she did not complain even when in dire need, the mission staff were concerned and alarmed. "She must be ill," they said, "very ill indeed, or she would not have written to tell us. She never makes much of hardships and sickness, she bears without complaint." Dr. Laws made enquires, and after hearing the reports of the missionaries, said, "No wonder she is ill." He ascertained that while keeping watch lest the innocent should die, Miss Slessor had been told that there was no milk for the babies. Worn out by her long vigil, her nerves strained by the suspense and watchfulness, she had left Okoyong by night, and had stumbled along the rough roads through the dripping thickets in darkness until five o'clock in the morning, when she reached Creek Town. Her clothes were wet through and she was exhausted. A change of garments was supplied, and she was put to bed, the tins of milk packed up, and then at 7 o'clock she started for Okoyong, this time in a canoe. She reached home without her absence being detected, and her patience, by the blessing of God, secured the deliverance of the victims.

Dr. Laws was large-hearted and large-minded too,

and he was therefore able to appreciate the independence and devotion of this brave woman. Without delay he started by canoe for Okoyong. Leaving Creek Town at nine o'clock, for a while the voyage was without incident. Then came a change of weather. During the three months of his stay at Calabar there were only five days at all fine. Now there swept down a fierce tornado of wind and rain. The river was lashed into fury, and swelled and rolled in wild waves under the deluge of rapid rain. Experienced traveller as he was, and well used to the water, Dr. Laws had never encountered such a tempest. The river immediately before him was concealed by the veil of fierce rain. But the canoe rode through it all, its course being onward to where Miss Slessor lay ill. It was late tea time when the canoe grounded on the beach. Then after he had set foot on the bank there lay a tramp of three miles through the forest before he reached the humble abode of the sufferer. His approach was noticed, and with courtesy Ma rose from her bed, and in her nightdress staggered to meet and greet her visitor. The doctor, kind and skilful, was a man with a will of his own. He asked, "What is this? Away to your bed at once." Ma, not accustomed to be ordered about or commanded, looked at the honest, manly face, and at once did as she was bidden. He prescribed for her, and then returned by night to Creek town. He had but just retired to rest when tidings came that his missionary cousin was ill. Off started Dr. Laws, but his skill was of no avail, the missionary died—the seventh martyr within eighteen months.

For those who die from privation, sickness or over-strain for God are as truly martyrs as those who are speared or burnt to death. It is the spirit and motive that count. If there be true devotion to the Lord Jesus Christ, a consecration of all the powers to Him and His service and a firm determination to refuse to disobey His orders, there is the true martyr spirit. Yes, the noble army of martyrs has many a brave boy and loving girl who has suffered derision, pain, and loss for the Saviour. At home, at school, it is necessary for peace of mind to avow one's faith, but sometimes sneers, cold contempt and cutting mockery will be the consequence of such showing one's colours.

It appears at times as if there is an especial hatred on the part of wicked people for those who avow themselves followers of the Saviour. Timid, sensitive souls shrink from this ordeal and suffer intensely, the while they continue faithful.

But to endure hardness is a duty, and our Lord has told us to expect the treatment He received, but then we have His promise to help us and to give us the victory.

Of Miss Slessor Dr. Laws formed a high opinion, one well deserved. He said, "She is a bit of a character. What a Salvation Army lass is to the Church at home, so is Miss Slessor to the Mission. She does a certain kind of work in a certain kind of way. I would not commend her as a pattern to others, but she has saved lives as no other man or woman could have dared to do. Had a man attempted to do what she had done during the recent riot he would have had his throat cut."

Her friends at home did not forget her. They sent money and boxes of gifts. These were distributed at times in a way that would have amused the senders. Thus a chief who sat in Mary Slessor's court received the gift of a dressing gown, and wore it as a state robe. Another dusky noble donned a white shirt as if it were a court robe. The amazement of the women at the delicate baby clothes was an education to the women, whose dusky babies crawled about the mud innocent of clothing and needing none.

For it is ever true that the people of Africa were not like the people of Scotland, who for centuries had enjoyed definite Gospel teaching, and continued faithful testimony to the truths contained in the Bible creates an atmosphere in the home, which restrains, and perhaps stimulates, life in its plastic years. These Africans whose past was one of bloodshed, hatred and filth, enjoyed the sermons they heard, and prayed with definite earnestness, but being liable to change they with the Gospel blended their drunken and wicked habits.

At times Mary Slessor felt the poorness of returns as they appeared in the Missionary Magazine, and asked herself, "Is the labour lost? A thousand times no." Many influences and different workers co-operate in the salvation of a nation, and the education of a down-trodden people means much silent work and perhaps many secret tears.

Christian workers are peculiarly liable to be discouraged. The Sunday School Class is so irresponsive, but who knows what is passing in the breast of a boy who is afraid to speak about what he does not quite understand. Let us have faith in our message, and believe that Jesus lifted up will draw old and young to faith in Him.

Hence, Mary Slessor, vaccinated when smallpox ravaged the district—listened to the troubles and disagreements of different tribes, the while dropping words that could never die, because of the Christ who gave them.

Especially did she love to gather her family for worship. She herself played the tambourine, now and then tapping on the head some heedless or inattentive girl. Troubled with persistent fever, and worn out by sleeplessness "Ma," was happy with her bairns. With them Sunday was a grand day. She would gather them round a long table, the smaller children happy on the floor the while she dispensed the sweets and other dainties that came from Scotland.

It was a memorable day when Janie, her chief helper, married before the chief, a young man—the first Christian marriage in her circle. They did not live happily ever after, for Janie soon left her spouse, and came back to "Ma" and took up her old duties.

Think of the tax upon a weary woman when a man burst in to say that his wife had given birth to twins and now lay neglected in a forest twelve miles distant. A tempest was gathering, but they pushed their way through the tangle, and found the woman lying upon the earth surrounded by charms. At first the husband refused, but at length consented to make a stretcher, and so through the darkness they stumbled along to home. Having carried the poor creature so far the husband and his man made off, leaving Miss Slessor to construct a hut to shelter her from the storm. So wearied was Miss Slessor that she lay down on the floor in her wet and muddy garments, too tired to wash or undress and fell asleep.

Now and then a ray of light shot across the dark sky, as when seven of her children were baptized, and when forty converts sat down together at the table of the Lord. This latter incident so pleased her that she exclaimed "I am sure our Lord will never keep it from my mother."

A lady writer in the *Morning Post*, who met her at the Governor's house, tells us of Miss Slessor that, "she was a woman close on sixty, with a heavily lined face and a skin from which the freshness and bloom had long ago departed; but there was fire in her old eyes still tired though they looked; there was sweetness and firmness about her lined mouth. Heaven knows who dressed her. She wore a skimpy tweed skirt, and a cheap nun's veiling blouse, and on her iron-grey hair was perched rakishly a forlorn broken picture hat of faded green chiffon with a knot of bright red to give the bizarre touch of colour she had learned to admire among her surroundings. 'Ye'll excuse my hands,' she said, and she held them out.

"They were hardened and roughened by work, work in the past, and they were just now bleeding from work finished but now; the skin of the palms was gone, the nails were worn to the quick; that they were painful there could be no doubt, but she only apologised for their appearance. After talking about the hard lot of women in Calabar and all Nigeria, she said with a touch of the sadness all tired workers feel :—'My time has been wasted. The puir bairns. They'd be better dead.'

"Her scarred hands fumbled with her dress, her tired eyes looked out into the blazing tropical sunshine, her lips quivered as she summed up her life's work. 'Failed, failed,' she cried. All that she had hoped, all that she had prayed for, nothing for herself had she ever sought except the power to help these children, and she felt that she had not helped them. They would be better dead.

"But the Commissioner did not think she had failed. Is the victory always to the strong?

" 'She has influence and weight,' he said. 'She can go where no white man dare go. She can sway the people when we cannot sway them. Because of her they are not so hard on the twins and their mothers as they used to be, no she has not failed.' "

The Commissioner was right. The people of Ibi-bio, troubled by the head hunters, sullen and cowed, a nation where the youth went naked next came under her sway.

One man told her that he had a son, who had learned to read, and whom he had hoped would become a teacher but he had died. The disconsolate father wailed out, "I want God, and you will not leave me till I've found Him." "Oh, father, God is here," was the answer, "He is waiting for you."

As we have said the condition of women was naturally a subject upon which she could speak. A man struck his wife with a hatchet because she had insulted him by stumbling against his black body.

It had actually grown up to be a law, that a girl not

ON AN OPEN LAKE

attached to a man could be insulted with impunity and the degrading serfdom.

A friend gave her £20, and with it she purposed founding a rest house for missionary ladies. It is related that while resident there Miss Slessor received a visitor who must needs leave early on the following morning. There were no clocks or watches but with ready resource Miss Slessor managed the business. She caught a cockerel and tied him to her bedpost. He lustily announced the dawn in time for the traveller to make a start.

The taking over of the country by the British was a boon to the missionaries. Not only was there a determined attempt to put down slavery, murder, and introduce the arts of peace, but new roads were made and motor cars ran along what was at one time a mere bush track.

The Government motor car which travelled to and from the Interior country had a white chauffeur who had a native assistant. This assistant who came from Lagos fell in love with Mary, one of Miss Slessor's girls. The marriage ceremony took place before the District Commissioner in his court. After this came the religious service, and after this a wedding breakfast. The head of the table was taken by an aged man, who, although a Mohammedan, had attended the services held by "Ma." To her he said, "Only God can make you such a mother and helper to everybody." This tribute coming from one who was not a Christian is a striking proof of what God did by the servant, in whose heart He abode.

After this pleasing incident came one of even greater

cheer. The Word of the Lord by her found lodgement in many hearts, and a Baptismal and Communion service lifted Mary's heart up to heaven. At Christmas she received the present of a new cycle, and then came the tribulation that always follows success. The bright sunshine is pleasant but it is by the dark days and moments of realized weakness that God most enriches and sanctifies the heart. After the darkness had warmed into mellow dawn, Miss Slessor used her returning strength to make journeys into the unexplored regions seeking to establish schools, and open the region to the Gospel.

She felt as did Michael Faraday, who was found by his friend, Sir Henry Acland weeping, his head bowed over an open Bible. "I fear you are feeling worse," said Sir Henry. "No," answered Faraday, "it is not that; but why—oh why will not men believe the blessed truths here revealed to them."

A like delight in the blessings Jesus gives to every forgiven sinner, and a deep and fervent affection for Him filled Mary Slessor with a longing that these delights should be made known to others, who wallowed in sin, and found nothing but increasing misery in the indulgence of their evil likings and doings.

Surely this is rational; it is the way to win souls for Christ. If you are saved seek to lead others to the Cross. Tell them of Jesus the mighty to save. The idle, careless, and hostile are not beyond the power of Jesus; at any rate, seek to win and save them.

Said a Scottish Minister, "I have an inscription which I should like to see hung over every home, over every heart, over every church: "How much owest thou unto my Lord?"   Hang this inscription up where you can daily see it, and while you can never repay the debt that you owe you can seek to show your sense of gratitude by telling about Jesus and His wondrous redemption, the tenderness of His love and His willingness to save.

CHAPTER V.

A Poor Woman who was Enriched by what she gave Above; a Sure Method of Securing True Wealth.

Dear Master mine! One prayer the last,
  Vouchsafe this grace to me;
A childlike heart of love, made strong
  By love's necessity.

Those who entirely to their God belong,
Those only can be wise, and pure and strong.
Lord help me lest when Thou dost claim my heart
I keep back doubting just one little part,
Help me O God, to give to thee the whole
The infinite surrender of the soul.

IT is said that the other day a tramp entering a casual ward took his seat on one of the benches. An old, sick man asked him, "Where do you come from?" "I come from the country." "From which county?" "I come from Kent.." "Oh that is my county. How did it look when you left it?" "Well, there was rain over the country but there was a rainbow too." Said the sick man, "Thank you. I wanted a word of comfort and you have given it me'.'

This was Miss Slessor's feeling about the next district she proposed to invade with the Gospel. There was rain, and darkness and shame, but over it was a rainbow upon which she read, "Ask of me and I will give thee the heathen for thine inheritance, and the uttermost parts of the earth for thy possession."

A troop that had attacked the British soldiers came to her to ask what they should do to appease the forces they could not resist. More than one interview took place, and in the end she went to Ikpe a town farther up the Creek. There four nations thronged the market, their language and conduct being abominable. Yet in this centre of evil some forty disciples were found. They had commenced to build a small house of prayer. Although she was in such a weak state, that any exertion was painful, Mary Slessor conveyed some leading officials of her Society to the selected spot, and they agreed with her as to the wisdom of her choice.

After this journey Miss Slessor was so ill that she could not land, but spent the night in her canoe although so near her home. But the converts at Ikpe continued to plead with her to come to their assistance. She took with her (for she could not deny this cry from Macedonia), iron and other essentials for house building.

Her courage was soon put to the test. Into a mob where swords as well as sticks were being freely used, she trust herself, and soon restored order and some kind of peace. Then when Government agents, protected by an armed guard, came to vaccinate the people there was a wild tumult. She undertook the task herself, and for weeks was employed as public vaccinator. The strain, the necessary visits to use her head-quarters, shook her slight frame, but she took laudanum, lay down in the canoe, and rose for further services.

Then there came welcome reinforcements, including medical men, who were of great assistance to her and to the mission. In course of time, finding that she did not improve as rapidly as he desired, the doctor transferred her to Use, and there he watched her with the viligance of love until she was quite well. The moment he released her, Mary was off to Ikpe, and was warmly welcomed by all the district.

The cycle being no longer suitable for her to use on account of her weakness, the ladies of a Glasgow church sent her a basket chair, which could be pushed or pulled by two boys. The chair was a great comfort; she rode in it and inspected sites and openings for schools, for her dream was of a vast army of Christians covering the whole of the district.

When she completed her three-times twelve years as a missionary, she humbly said, "I'm lame and feeble and foolish; the wrinkles are wonderful—no concertina was ever so wonderfully folded and convoluted. I'm a wee, wee wifie, verra little buikit—but I grip on well none-the-less."

A medical friend said with pathetic humour, "You are a strong woman Ma. You ought to have been dead by ordinary rule long ago—any one else would." The explanation of her success and continued vitality was the secret of a college friend of whom Dr. Hutton writes : This man suffered from an affection of the heart which well nigh terminated his earthly service. He struggled for health, but found that there was a point in the quadrangle of the University, which he could not bring himself to pass. Day by day he drew near to the point, setting himself to face the difficulty but as often as he did so, it was as if his heart would stop for ever; he had to lean for support against the wall. Then he opened his heart to his friend. He confessed that he knew quite well that until he could pass that difficult point he could not go outside the college and face the task of a man. His brother listened and then said, "Fred give me your hand." The two of them went past that dizzy point. Said the friend, "Come, let us go past it again and again," and they did so, all fear oozing away from the sick man's mind. This was the case with frail, strong Mary Slessor. Some One held her hand, and so it was that by His grace she went among savage tribes who welcomed her and listened to her message, and from loving her came to love her Saviour.

Is it not wise to secure such a friend, to have Him with us who can guide us past the danger points, make darkness light, and crooked places plain before us? Make friends at once with the Lord Jesus Christ, and then you would never be alone and are bound to succeed.

A lady of Scotland knowing the frail health of this wonderful missionary and realising that Caledonia was too cold for her at this time arranged for a holiday at the Canary Islands. Taking Janie with her, the wee

E

woman went to the Canaries, treated on the journey
with the respect that true holiness and consecration to
Christ brings. She made her way once more through
the Bible, the while she enjoyed sun, sea, and flowers.
Among the guests at the hotel she won many friends,
and convinced others of the value of Foreign Missions.

She returned to Africa renewed in spirit and in
body, and at once plunged into work with the enthusiasm of a girl. And there to the last lap of her race
friends gathered around her, realising how precious
she was to them. Government officials living hard
lives came to see her, the instructions from Headquarters were, to assist her in every possible way, not
only because of her value to the State as a peace-
maker, but because of her own high qualities. A large
place must be assigned to prayer in her mental outfit,
for she realised it as the potent force by which God
is brought into touch with human need and weakness.

Mr. James H. Smith of Dundee compiled a book
which ran through many editions, and we believe is still
in demand, *"Our Faithful God: Answers to Prayer."*
To him when he asked for her testimony to be in-
cluded in this useful book she thus unveiled the secrets
of her heart and work :—"My life is one long daily,
hourly record of answered prayer. For physical health,
for mental overstrain, for guidance given marvellously,
for errors and dangers averted, for enmity to the
Gospel subdued, for food provided at the exact hour
needed, for everything that goes to make up life,
and my poor service, I can testify with a full and often
wonder-stricken awe, that I believe God answers
prayer. I know God answers prayer. I have proved

through long decades while alone, as far as man's help and presence are concerned, that God answers prayer. Cavilings, logical or physical, are of no avail to me. It is the very atmosphere in which I live, and breathe, and have my being, and it makes life glad and free, and a million times worth living. I can give no other testimony. I am sitting here alone on a log among a company of natives. My children, whose very lives are a testimony that God answers prayer, are working around me. Natives are crowding past on the beach road to attend palavers, and I am at perfect peace, far from my own countrymen and conditions, because I know God answers prayer. Food is scarce just now. We live from hand to mouth. We have not more than will be our breakfast to-day, but I know we shall be fed, for God answers prayer."

To Mary Slessor prayer was as habitual as breathing, and at times almost as unconscious. Thus, when wearied with a journey, she sat down to a meal, she simply said, "Thank ye, Father, ye ken I'm tired." When her eye-glasses were lost, she asked, "O, Father, give me back my spectacles," and they were found. And as she ploughed her way through the tangle of the bush road, having no one else with her, she talked to her Father who was near her, and the habit filled her with a deep sense of God and some of His power. Years ago there lived a poet, Johnnie Donne. In his early days he sported as a crest a sheaf of snakes. This symbolized the temptations he felt in his heart. But he came to know the Lord Jesus Christ as a Saviour, and he at once assumed a new crest. The sheaf of snakes disappeared, and in its place he put

Christ crucified, Christ crucified against the background
of an archer. Which crest is yours? If Christ is
yours then you have an anchor that cannot fail, and
will by it be drawn within the veil, whither the Fore-
runner is for us entered.

Being a devout believer in prayer as a habit of daily
life, Mary Slessor had of course a deep acquaintance
with the Bible. Not that she merely knew the order
of the books, or some verses plucked here and there.
She worked her way steadily through the Bible, mark-
ing in the margin the lessons the passages taught, and
the blessing she had received. Thus somehow the Bible
entered into her very being, and she was suffused with
its spirit and power. The Bible Society's Colporteur
at Port Said tells us that he boarded a ship, and on
the lower deck found a German seaman sweeping out
a cabin. He was depressed, and in course of con-
versation he and the Colporteur disputed which was
the greater sinner. "What," the German exclaimed,
"you are the first man to tell me that he is a greater
sinner than I am." Taking a Gospel from the Colporteur, he began to read. "Ah," he exclaimed, "that
I were a little child again, and could read it with a
clean heart." His shipmates interposed, "Is that you,
Jansen," they said, "what wonder has happened to
you?" "No wonder at all," the man replied, " I want
to sweep out my heart, and I am buying a broom."

The influence of a prayerfully studied Bible is first
this. It does cleanse the heart, and by it there comes
gracious influences that check and prompt, for the
Holy Spirit has a special charge of the Bible. Never
mind if it appears dry. Read it. No matter if you

think you know all about it.   Read it and you will
find rest to you soul, because it will point you to Jesus
and lead you to His gracious feet.

One visit Mary Slessor paid that was a source of
intense pleasure to her.   She went back to Akpap, and
preached to over 400 professing Christians.   And it
must be confessed that to come out as an avowed believer in Christ in the presence of hostile heathenism
costs something.

Sir Frederick Lugard, when Governor General of
Nigeria, brought Miss Slessor's services to Royal
notice.   The communication came before the Chapter-
General of the Order of the Hospital of St. John of
Jerusalem.   The King is Sovereign Head of the Chap-
ter and the Duke of Connaught Grand Prior.   Miss
Slessor was elected an Honorary Associate, and received a Maltese Cross in Silver to be worn on the
left shoulder.   This was publicly presented to her at
Calabar.   Her testimony was, "If I have done anything in my life it has been easy, because the Master
has gone before."

Tidings of her honour came home, and before long
Ma found herself famous all over the world among
those who love the Lord Jesus and labour for the
extension of the Kingdom.

Soon after this she had at Ikpe to encounter determined opposition.   The chief had taken offence because
some girls had begun to attend Gospel services.   The
girls were flogged, and forced to take part in heathen
practices.   Miss Slessor had a struggle with the chief,
for the forces of evil are mighty, and the Devil never
leaves until he is driven out.   In the end the Gospel

conquered so far that the girls were allowed to attend her services. But upon the question of the survivor of one of twins there was a determined stand. Ten weeks of ardent conflict ensued, and at last there was a giving way of native prejudice, and the child was taken to its parents, but only to die. The tender mercies of the wicked are indeed cruel, and Satan is the ruin of hard hearts.

Then Miss Slessor went to the end of the New Road, and took possession of the Rest House there. She made up her mind to have a gipsy picnic. Thus she herself slept in a camp-bed, which was borrowed; her girls lay on the mud floor among the lizards. Some pots and pans were borrowed from her neighbours. A tin of fat, some salt and pepper, tea and sugar, and roasted plantain did duty as bread. As to washing day, one article at a time was left off and washed in an iron pail, and then dried in the sun. While here Miss Slessor began to invite the converts within reach to visit her, but she found that twin trouble was an effectual barrier to their coming. She gradually, by tact and patience, wore some of the prejudices away, but prejudice lives long and dies but slowly. In the end she secured a footing in the district, and in due time a mission house was prepared. One by one these closed villages opened their doors to her, and into them she rushed with eager glee and haste to save.

The erection of the house at Odoro Ikpe proved an exhaustive task to her, already weakened as she was by long years of hardship and privation. And a feeling of isolation, a sense of loneliness, often crept over her, as it did with John Wesley when he heard of

the death of his brother Charles, and with tears gave
out the hymn—

> My company before has gone,
> And I am left alone with Thee.

Then came the Great War with its world-wide up-
heaval. The opening days of the conflict were a pain
to her. She was shocked at the success of the
Germans, although she always rested on the grand
assertion of the Psalm, "The Lord Reigneth."

On the 8th of January, fever again laid hold of
her, and in spite of all that love could do to detain
her, she slipped away into the blessed arms of Him
who was once nailed to the tree. Dr. Stalker, in his
Trial and Death of Jesus Christ, tells the following
story, which he vouches for. A private diary says,
"I remember when I was a student visiting a dying
man. He had been in the University with me, but a
few years ahead; and at the close of a brilliant career
in college he was appointed to a professorship of
philosophy in a Colonial University. But after a few
years he fell into bad health, and he came home to
Scotland to die. It was a summer Sunday afternoon
when I called to see him, and it happened that I was
able to offer him a drive. His great frame was with
difficulty got into the carriage, but then he lay back
comfortably and was able to enjoy the fresh air. Two
other friends were with him that day—college com-
panions who had come out from the city to visit him.
On the way back they dropped into the rear and I
was alone beside him, when he began to talk with
appreciation of their friendship and kindness. "But,"

he said, "do you know what they have been doing all
day?" I could not guess. "Well, they have been
reading to me *Sartor Resartus*, and oh, I am awfully
tired of it." Then turning on me his large eyes he
began to repeat, "This is a faithful saying, and worthy
of all acceptation, that Christ Jesus came into the
world to save sinners, of whom I am chief"; and
then he added with great earnestness, "There is nothing else of any use to me now." So Mary Slessor
believed and nothing else was worth telling to the
blacks she loved. For life, for death, this is all that
is of use, and it never fails.

> Oh make but trial of His love,
> Experience will decide
> How blest are they, and only they
> Who in the Lord confide.

The weeping and wailing of the girls whom she had
rescued and nurtured to happy, holy usefulness awoke
the village, and the natives, both men and women,
hurried to the house, whence this saint had ascended
to heaven. The weeping of these black folk betokened
the deep respect and affection Mary Slessor had in-
spired; not only had she been a ruler, she had also
been a mother to all who were in need or sorrow.

Burial in the East is speedy. The coffin with the
precious remains was taken by launch to Duke Town,
and there, with tears and rejoicings, they buried all
that was mortal of Mary Slessor. The alert, eager
presence was withdrawn from Calabar, but the words
she uttered and the deeds she had wrought remained
to testify of her that the Lord had wrought great
things by her.

Dr. Alexander Whyte, referring to the day when the decision against the Free Church of Scotland was given in the House of Lords, says, "When I staggered down the fatal stair and came into the lobby in the House of Lords, I found my friend here—shall I call him my father or my brother? I am getting so old now, I will call him my brother—there he was walking about the lobby with his splendid serenity. Men said, 'Have you seen Rainy? How is he taking it?' And the answer was, 'As smiling and happy as ever,' And why? Because he has been long years rooted in God; he is an experienced Christian man." Yes, it dawned upon many who had grown familiar with the presence now withdrawn, that Mary Slessor had been long years deeply rooted in God, and had become an experienced Christian, and that directed the thinker to the Giver of her qualities and the Doer of her works. The sorrow of many nations, human if black, brought her character in full view, and it was seen that in her was the very likeness of the Lord Jesus Christ. Mary Slessor's heart had been deeply wrung by the sorrows of women under savage rule. Custom compelled a woman to belong to some chief or man, otherwise she could be insulted or even maltreated with impunity. To provide for these poor women, she had planned a settlement, where agriculture could be a means of support, while other industries might be encouraged.

It was resolved that this longing of hers should be gratified, and a Home for Women and Girls was opened.

Her native land was not far behind in honouring this brave Scotch Lassie.

Extract from "Courier," 29th Sept., 1923.

TO THE MEMORY OF A GREAT WOMAN.

DUNDEE'S TRIBUTE TO MARY SLESSOR.
STAINED GLASS WINDOWS UNVEILED.

Two artistic stained glass windows in memory of Mary Slessor, the Dundee factory girl who became a distinguished African Missionary, were unveiled in the Albert Institute, Dundee, yesterday afternoon.

Designs of the windows were received from artists in Edinburgh, Birmingham, Glasgow, and London, and the committee's choice ultimately fell upon that submitted by Mr. William Aikman, London.

The two principal subjects of the memorial are Mary Slessor at a loom and in the African Mission field. Outstanding incidents in her life at home and amongst the savage tribes of the Dark Continent are depicted by 20 pictures which form the lower part and the border of the windows.

Very early in the afternoon people began to flock to the Victoria Art Galleries, where the ceremony was held. Arrangements had been made for receiving a gathering of about 450, but long before half-past two o'clock, the hour of the ceremony, that number had been greatly exceeded, and the passages and doorways were crowded with men and women desirous of paying homage to the memory of a wonderful woman. Ex-Lord Provost Longair, who presided, was accompanied to the platform by many of the city ministers,

BURNING THEIR FETISHES

Dr. J. T. T. Ramsay. Mayor of Blackburn, a personal friend of Mary Slessor during her early days in Dundee, and Mr. W. P. L. Livingstone, the author of "Mary Slessor in Calabar." The Mayor told of how Mary Slessor and he in 1863, were among the Sunday School children of Dundee who collected money to build the missionary ship, the *John Williams,* as a memorial of the Martyr of Erromanga. Then he spoke of her work in the Cowgate, of her studies at the night school, of her home duties, where she was scrupulously clean, painstaking and thrifty, and of the steady development of her personality in her fight against the heavy odds of her early life.

Prayer was offered by Rev. J. Sinclair, Lundie, Moderator of Dundee Presbytery. The Chairman explained the origin of the memorial scheme, and said he had been told that Dundee had never done itself justice in not in some way commemorating the mill girl missionary—Mary Slessor. Accordingly steps were taken to rectify the ommission, and a committee was formed for the purpose of setting up a suitable, worthy, practical and pictorial memorial. The figure of Mary Slessor was one which appealed greatly to the young, and as a result many of the subscriptions had come from children. He wanted to place on record the committee's appreciation of the generosity of Baxter Bros., Ltd., in whose establishment Mary Slessor worked. who had given a donation of £100. (Applause).

Rev. Dr. Adam Philip stated it was a matter of legitimate pride that their little Scotland had done so much to open up Africa, a country which had gained

so much through the work of men like Mungo Park
and David Livingstone and women like Mary Slessor
in whom the first note of religion was love, and who
set forth to apply the principals of the Gospel to the
healing of the open sores of Africa.

There never was a stranger and more touching story
than that of Mary Slessor. They had just seen a great
land—Japan—almost laid prostrate in a moment by
a touch of the hand of God. In Mary Slessor they
had seen one of the fragile and weakest things of
the earth touched by the same great hand and lifted
up into power, and through God's gentleness made
great. (Applause).

Principal Rev. J. K. Macgregor, Calabar, said the
doctrine of Mary Slessor's courage was her faith in
God. She believed that God reigns, and that in her
missionary work He was at all times behind her with
His unlimited resources. The secret of her power
over the natives was that she appealed to the best in
them, and they gave her the best they had. In truth,
she was a great Christian saint, and a great Christian
woman.

Mr. Livingstone said it astonished him to see how
quickly Mary Slessor's fame had spread throughout
the world. His book dealing with her life had been
translated into many foreign languages, and he had
just received that week a request to allow it to be
printed in Braille for the use of the blind.

Dr. Ramsay gave a comprehensive resumé of Mary
Slessor's early life in Dundee, and said she was
brought up to be diligent, scrupulously clean, pains-

taking in everything she attempted to do, and thrifty.

Mr. T. M. Davidson, who acted as secretary of the Memorial Committee, then left the hall, and accompanied by six members of the platform party, proceeded to the ground floor of the Museum, where he formally unveiled the windows. On the party's return to the Galleries, the Chairman handed the Memorial over to the care of the Albert Institute Committee.

In accepting the responsibility on behalf of the Committee, ex-Bailie J. H. Martin, said the words used in Motley's "Dutch Republic" regarding William Prince of Orange, were just as applicable to Mary Slessor—"so long as he lived he was the guiding star of a whole and brave nation, and when he died the little children cried in the streets."

And now, all that remains for us to do is to remember that Mary Slessor was great because she had no cheap ambitions and mean ideals. Her aims were great because they were given her by the Lord Jesus Christ. She made much of Him, and He made her like Himself, and by her did His will. "Go thou and do likewise."

One thing ought to be remembered, and that was that Mary Slessor was naturally timid. She was afraid of cows and hesitated before crossing a street. She dreaded crowds, and yet she faced hordes of murderous savages and led them to Christ. She had but little schooling, but in the spare moments of her lonely life she acquired much knowledge, and every kind of knowledge enriched her mind. Thus, one day while walking with a visitor he complained of toothace.

Mary stopped and plucked a flower and gave it to him. "Chew that," said she, "and your toothache will go." He found her words true, and plucked a flower for a second dose. She stopped him saying, "If you eat that in less than five minutes you will die. It is poison."

But quite apart from her study and industry there was the Lord Jesus Christ. Lord Cairns (whom a friend called "the central calm") bore public testimony that "The Lord Jesus Christ does satisfy even here when we are in full communion with Him," and this was the secret of Mary Slessor's happiness, ability and success.

It may be ours too. At home, at school, in the preparation for life's work, as well as while discharging its tasks, remember Jesus. Of the gifted Miss Marsh, her grand-neice tells us that "the source and secret of her strength was her vivid realization of the Personal Friendship of the Lord Jesus Christ." To Him she confided everything, and she added, "He never repents."

This experience may be yours. You have but to say "Yes" to His call. Trust Him and then treat Him as a friend. He will be one if you will but allow Him the first place in your heart and life. And who can tell what He will do for you and do by you?

A Mr. Wishard of America, while in Turkey before the War, said to an Armenian priest, "Why has your church lost the enthusiasm for souls that characterized it in the early centuries, when its members went everywhere active in telling men of Christ?"

"We aren't an educated people," the priest made answer.

"What evidence have we that the godly witnesses who were so successful were educated men?" asked Mr. Wishard.

The priest evaded this enquiry remarking, "We have no railroad facilities as you have in America, and so are handicapped in our work."

Mr. Wishard persisted, "What railroads had they in the first century?"

The priest then said, "Ah, brother, those men had a relation with God and the Holy Spirit which we do not have."

Yes, and for lack of that relation the Armenian Church decayed and lost power, as will every body of Christians and every Christian too. We must be filled and guided and controlled by the Holy Spirit.

A lady, who was upheld by the Holy Spirit, once spied a man at the top of a very high ladder in a dangerous position. She stood still and prayed that he might get to the ground safely, and when he stood upon the earth told him that she had prayed for him, told him too about Jesus and then bade him farewell. Eleven years after this incident she heard about this bricklayer. As she went away the man said to himself, "Can a stranger care to pray for me and I never pray for myself?" He began to pray, and before long became not only a true Christian but one eager to win others to trust and love his Saviour.

First Andrew came to Jesus, and then he found his brother and brought him also to the Lord. No one is too young, too uneducated for the Saviour to accept

and use, and once united to Him by faith and love
His power will act through all one is and does, and
who can tell what blessing may follow.

To think His thoughts is blessedness supreme,
  To know HIMSELF, the Thinker is our life;
To rest this weary intellect on His
  Is the glad ending of mind's endless strife.

      So shall success be mine in spite
        Of feebleness in me;
      Beyond all disappointment then
        And failure I shall be.
      The work is Thine, not mine, O Lord,
        It is Thy race we run;
      Give light! and then shall all I do
        Be well and truly done.

THE END.